SHAKE IT UP

SHAKE IT UP

COCKTAILS
INSPIRED BY THE MUSIC OF
TAYLOR SWIFT

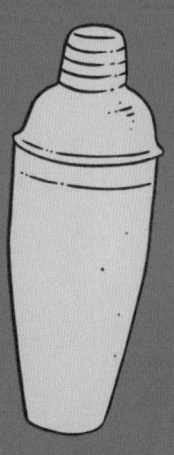

ILLUSTRATIONS BY
LAURÈNE BOGLIO

WELBECK

CONTENTS

INTRODUCTION

Fancy a Swift drink? Look no further than this handy cocktail book inspired by our favourite pop princess. With a walk through her incredible 20-year career, each cocktail is inspired by a different Taylor Swift song, with ingredients to match, giving you the perfect companion drinks for your TS playlist.

Soak up the stunning flavours and marvel in the heady aromas as you test out the recipes, carefully chosen to pair with the spirit and soul of the music.

As any devoted Swiftie appreciates, Taylor's genius is not just reflected in the scorching lyrics of her break-up and revenge songs, or the catchy tunes that mean they go straight to the head and heart. The Pennsylvania-born singer-songwriter has also revolutionized the music industry, taking on the powers that be and standing up against the exploitation of artists on all levels. A born fighter, she also spreads love and devotion to her fans and frequently reaches out to help those in need, with personal acts of generosity as well as the sterling work of her own foundation. Tay is also one of the hardest-working music acts, penning over 220 banging tunes since 2006 and re-recording many of her early albums in a bid to regain control of her back catalogue.

Taylor's stellar career continues to smash records and on 27 October 2023 she became the most-streamed artist in a single day in Spotify history. She followed that at the 2024 Grammys by making history once again when she became the first artist to win four Best Album gongs, picking up the award for *Midnights* after three previous wins for *Fearless*, *1989* and *folklore*. Now if that doesn't deserve a cocktail toast, we don't know what does.

But, between studio sessions, Taylor loves to let her hair down and what she knows, better than anyone, is that heartaches and break-ups should always be addressed by gathering the girl squad and embarking on an epic night out, with cocktails an absolute must. When any member of the Swift Squad is down in the dumps, heartbreak queen Taylor is on hand with a shoulder to cry on, a carefully worded piece of advice... and a classic cocktail shaker.

Taylor herself is a huge fan of mixology, being credited with single-handedly bringing back the Cosmopolitan when she was spotted ordering several of the cocktail, made famous by *Sex and the City*'s Carrie Bradshaw, in a New York bar. More recently she switched her allegiance to the French Blonde, with her new drink of choice featuring a delicious mix of gin, the aperitif Lillet, St-Germain elderflower liqueur and grapefruit juice. News that she couldn't get enough of the heady tipple, on a visit to a bar near Kansas City, caused the recipe to go viral. And cocktails even make it into her hit songs. She name-checks the classic recipes Old Fashioned and Island Breeze in the lyrics of her hits 'Getaway Car' and 'Ready For It?'. In 'You Need to Calm Down' she references people taking shots at her like it's tequila and in the *Midnights* album closer 'Mastermind', she refers to her part in a relationship as providing the 'liquor in our cocktails'.

Taylor's adopted home of New York – where she is occasionally spotted in the cocktail bars of Manhattan – is arguably the home of mixology. In 1806, The Balance and Columbian Repository of Hudson, New York was the first to define the modern-day cocktail as 'a stimulating liquor composed of any kind of sugar, water, and bitters.' It's also where many of the classics were created, including the Long Island Iced Tea, the Manhattan and the original Martini.

From the Bad Bloody Mary and the ME!jito, to the Look What You Made Me Brew, each of the delicious recipes in this book is inspired by the music of Taylor Swift, paying tribute to a remarkable career spanning two decades. Starting with the Tim McStraw, a nod to the first single which shot her to fame in 2006, the cocktails take a meander through her albums, from her self-titled debut to her 2022 opus *Midnights*. Like Taylor's uniquely personal lyrics, detailing her life, loves and friendship battles, they switch from the sweet to the bitter, hitting every note in between. While each one is inspired by the song title, the carefully blended mixture of ingredients also mirrors the tone of the lyrics, whether it be a triumphant celebration glass, bubbling with fizz, like the Starlight Spritz, a vibrant and intense blend mirroring those powerful feelings of love with Red Raspberry Martini, or a spine-tingling sour mix recalling unrequited love, like Lemon Drop on My Guitar.

The easy-to-mix recipes are in chronological order, as a mini(bar) tribute to Taylor's career, enabling you to taste your way through the eras. So, get the cocktail cabinet stocked, gather your squad, crank up the music and dance your way through the Taylor-made concoctions in celebration of the phenomenon who forever changed the world of pop. Forget the players, haters, heartbreakers and fakers... we're just gonna shake, shake, shake, shake, shake, shake it up!

THE BASICS

EQUIPMENT

You can make drinks with virtually no bar equipment, but it's difficult to make great drinks with little more than the basics. You don't need to transform your living room into a proper bar, but if you want to make a good impression then it's worth investing in the essentials: a shaker, for example, the right glasses, a good range of spirits, liqueurs and bitters. You'll want to know how to open a bottle of Champagne and how to cut a twist. In time you'll realize that what turns an ordinary drink into a work of art is simply attention to detail: using orange or Peychaud's bitters instead of Angostura, even just knowing how important good-quality ice is. Small and inexpensive touches that make all the difference.

COCKTAIL SHAKERS

Shakers come in a mass of shapes and sizes and while it might seem like a good idea to invest in a novelty one, run three simple checks before you part with your money. Firstly, is it easy to hold? It's pointless having a baroque instrument on the bar if you drop it all the time. Secondly, is it easy to use? Does the lid get stuck, or fall off, and can you strain easily? Thirdly, is it made from stainless steel or glass? If it isn't, don't buy it.

Many bartenders use a Boston shaker. This comes in two parts: one a tall thick glass, the other similarly shaped but slightly smaller and made of stainless steel. This part fits inside the top of the glass part, allowing you to shake the ice and liquid between the two. You can also use the glass part for stirring drinks and, because it's clear, it allows you to see if your proportions are correct. Be warned, Boston shakers can be tricky to separate.

JUGGLING

You may, in time, decide to try and copy that hotshot barkeep you saw working the crowd in Las Vegas with his juggling tricks. Our advice is DON'T. Flair bartending – as juggling bottles, glasses and shakers is known – is great fun to watch but, without wishing to be too much of a killjoy, the most important element in preparing a drink is making sure the drink is made correctly and tastes good. Anyway, it can make a dreadful mess of the carpet.

GLASSES

There are eight glass shapes
that are most widely used.

SHOT

It's fairly obvious what this glass is for. Small shots of the hard stuff intended to be drunk quickly, frozen vodka, tequila, etc. They can double up as measures if needed.

OLD FASHIONED

Great for the eponymous cocktail (or variants thereof) which can be built in the glass or for old-fashioned drinks like whisky and soda.

COLLINS (TALL)

The shape shows that this is a glass intended for long drinks, not just members of the Collins family but a Gin and Tonic is perfect in this as are Mojitos and Mint Juleps.

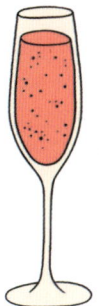

CHAMPAGNE FLUTE

The only glass for Champagne. Its shape encourages a regular, prolonged, stream of bubbles.

WINE GLASS

Red wines and great whites need to breathe in the glass to release its aroma. A wide-mouthed goblet not only does this but also allows you to swirl the wine to see the colour.

CHAMPAGNE SAUCER

Use this for any short mixed drink: Daiquiri, Sours, etc.

HIGHBALL

Use this for making long drinks, modern, fruity cocktails, Bloody Mary, etc.

MARTINI (COCKTAIL)

The classic shape for all short mixed drinks, such as Martini and Manhattan. Three rules:
(1) make sure they are cold;
(2) hold them by the stem while drinking
    (or the drink will heat up);
(3) buy smaller rather than larger examples.

BAR ACCESSORIES

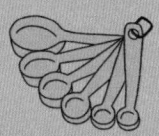

○ MIXING GLASS
This is an essential piece of kit you can't be without.

○ MEASURE
Use a measure until you feel confident to measure by eye.

○ MEASURING SPOONS
To gauge those vital small additions.

○ ICE BUCKET
Keep it full.

○ ICE SCOOP
To ladle in the ice when making frozen drinks.

○ STRAWS
These come in different lengths and widths, depending on the type of drink being served. They are necessary for longer drinks.

○ CHOPPING BOARD
Use as a preparation surface when making drinks, chopping up fruit, herbs and other garnishes.

○ SHARP KNIFE
Especially important for preparing garnishes.

○ COCKTAIL STICKS
Handy for securing olives, onions, cherries and other fruit.

○ SWIZZLE STICKS
Useful for stirring long drinks.

○ ICE TONGS
Use tongs instead of your hands to pick up ice, otherwise it will melt.

○ STRAINER
To ensure that no bits of ice end up in the drink.

BARTENDER'S CHECKLIST

ALCOHOL
- Gin (kept in fridge or freezer)
- Sloe gin
- Vodka (kept in fridge or freezer)
- Flavoured vodka
- White rum
- Gold/dark rum
- Tequila (100% blue agave silver/reposado)
- Bourbon
- Rye whiskey
- Cognac
- Apricot brandy
- Noilly Prat
- Sweet vermouth
- Chambéry vermouth
- Dry vermouth
- Cointreau/Curaçao
- Campari
- Green Chartreuse
- Kahlúa
- Champagne
- Aperol
- Angostura bitters
- Peychaud's bitters
- Selection of liqueurs (amaretto, crème de cacao/menthe, etc.)
- Mandarine Napoléon

OTHERS
- Fresh limes, lemons, oranges, grapefruit
- Coconut cream
- Grenadine
- Freshly squeezed fruit juices
- Purées (peach, banana, mango)
- Maraschino cherries
- Sugar and sugar cubes
- Salt
- Lime cordial
- Tabasco sauce
- Worcestershire sauce
- Gomme syrup
- Simple syrup
- Agave syrup
- Mixers (tonic, soda water, ginger ale)

MINIBAR SETUP

Once you've developed a passion for mixing drinks, the next thing you'll need is a home bar for assembling drinks. The days of improvising in the kitchen will become a thing of the past and you'll want to perform your mixing skills in front of your friends.

Not all of us have the space to dedicate a corner of a room, let alone an entire room, to mixing drinks. In any case, you can have as much fun making cocktails from a small cocktail cabinet. Look around in fleamarkets or antique shops for them; it is amazing what you can find. The key here is to choose your spirit brands carefully and only buy the spirits and liqueurs that you know you'll use regularly.

Because space is limited, restrict the number of spirits to those that work the best with the widest range of cocktails: a good-quality silver or reposado tequila will be more versatile than an expensive anejo, for example.

Store your most useful spirits in the cabinet along with your shaker, strainer, measures, and so on, and keep other less-used spirits and liqueurs close by in a cupboard where you keep your glasses. Store vodka and gin in the fridge so that you also have space in your cabinet for bitters, rum, bourbon/Scotch and tequila.

In a large home bar it is possible to mix a variety of different drinks for your guests, but with a smaller setup it might be best to decide what you are going to make and give everyone the same. It makes life easier and allows you to concentrate on the most important aspect of mixology, which is making a good drink. The downside of having a small bar is that it can take a little more time. If you are making a round of martinis, you'll have to go to the kitchen to get the ice, gin, vermouth and cold glasses, so ensure that these are all ready and waiting for collection before your guests arrive.

The last thing you want to be doing is rattling around in the fridge for that bottle of gin. Then, when you get back, you can amaze your friends with your dexterity.

STORAGE

Apart from having the right bottle in the right place at the right time, good storage also involves knowing the best way to preserve a drink's freshness and character.

SPIRITS

Spirits are less sensitive than wines, but even they have their own peculiarities. White spirits, especially vodka and gin, should be kept in the fridge, or better still in the freezer. The cold temperature gives them a rich texture and, since cocktails are cold drinks, improves the quality of your mixed drink. Remember to stick to brands at 40% ABV and above; anything below that will freeze.

Brown spirits, such as brandy, Scotch/bourbon and dark rum can be kept at room temperature. Unlike wine, spirits do not improve in the bottle, although there are some people who claim that Chartreuse does. Usually a spirit will start to deteriorate if the bottle has been opened months or years before. This is because when air is let into the bottle the spirit starts to oxidize, the aroma flattens and loses its vibrancy. If you do have a half-full bottle of precious malt, cognac or bourbon then simply decant it into a smaller bottle. Brown spirits in clear glass bottles will lose their colour if stored for long periods in direct sunlight.

WINE

Wine storage is a slightly more complex issue. Many wines will improve in the bottle and ideally should be stored in a cellar. That said, most of us tend to drink wine soon after we buy it, which is why many wines are made to be drunk when young. Speak to your wine merchant and find out what wines will benefit from some ageing: these will include quality claret, some Californian and Australian Cabernet and Merlot, Burgundy (red and white) top German Riesling, Loire Chenin Blanc and Cabernet Franc, Rhône reds, Chianti Riserva, Barolo/Barbaresco. The same goes for Champagne, including most non-vintage brands. It really is a good idea to buy Champagne by the case and store it for a few months.

IN THE UNLIKELY EVENT...

There are many devices available which aim to preserve wine, but if you are going to finish off a bottle the next night, just replace the cork in the bottle. The Vacu Vin system which sucks the air out of the bottle might save the wine from oxidizing but it also sucks the life and aroma out at the same time. Wine bars use a system which pumps nitrogen into the bottle, sealing it from the worst effects of the air, but while it is quite efficient this method is expensive.

There many myths about how to keep Champagne, such as putting a silver spoon in the neck of the bottle in order to preserve the bubbles. This is just a myth. Champagne should be sealed with a stopper and put in the fridge. The stopper won't prevent the gas from escaping – the bubbles remain in the wine for a day or so – but it does stop any odours from the fridge seeping into the wine.

TECHNIQUES

SHAKING

Shaking is the most effective way of mixing the ingredients, while simultaneously chilling the drink and diluting it slightly. Dilution helps to release flavours allowing them to blend together. Never fill the shaker more than halfway with ice. Shake the drink until the outside of the shaker is freezing to the touch. Cocktails should be very cold. Use ice cubes, not crushed ice, unless otherwise stated in the recipe because a drink shaken over crushed ice can quickly become too diluted.

STIRRING

Stirring is used to marry flavours which go together easily, without making the drink cloudy, which is what happens when you shake. The principle is the same as shaking: a way to mix the ingredients together, chill a drink quickly and dilute it slightly. Half fill a shaker with ice and stir for about 20 seconds, or until the outside is chilled, then strain into cocktail glasses. Some recipes, for example the Subourbon Legends (p. 102), suggest the drink is stirred in the serving glasses.

BLENDING

This is a good way to make long, thirst-quenching drinks. Simply whizz up the ice with the spirit ingredients and serve unstrained in the glass. Because the ice is crushed it melts more quickly and produces a fairly dilute alcoholic slush in the glass. It's a matter of personal preference. Some people like to taste the alcohol in the drink, but can also see the advantage of a frozen blended drink when you have a long, hot summer's afternoon ahead of you, hence the Frozen Daiquiri.

MUDDLING

Some recipes, such as Karma-pirinha, p. 166, and Old Style, p. 86, call for 'muddling' to take place. This involves pressing and mixing ingredients: mint, fruit, peel, etc., in the bottom of the glass, often with bitters and over sugar cubes. The rough surface of the sugar helps break up the ingredients easily. You can use the back of a spoon if you don't own a proper muddler.

LAYERING

This process involves introducing the heaviest part of the drink first, followed by a succession of progressively lighter layers. The layers are carefully poured to sit one on top of the other. (See Death by a Thousand Shots, p. 122).

SALTING AND SUGARING

The intention here is to coat the outside, not the inside, of the rim. Don't, therefore, bury the rim in a pile of salt or sugar. Instead, moisten the outside rim with lime or lemon juice and then carefully turn the glass, side on, in a saucer of salt or sugar. Alternatively, you can sprinkle the salt or sugar onto the rim while rotating the glass, although this is a messier method.

FRUIT

When using fruit for a garnish, make sure it is fresh and has been thoroughly washed. Try rolling limes and lemons before you cut them as this starts to release their juices. To cut a twist, pare small strips from a lemon ensuring there is some white pith attached. Holding the peel between thumb and forefinger give it a quick twist so that it sprays some of its oil on the surface of the drink. Run the twist round the rim of the glass and gently drop in.

FLAMING

The secret of flaming brandy is to warm the glass first, either over a hot coil on the stove or by holding it under a hot tap. Pour in the brandy and ignite. To light absinthe, or high-proof vodka, hold the flame at the edge of the glass until the alcohol catches. Be aware that the flames can flare up, so ensure that your hair is not hanging over the glass.

FLAVOURED SPIRITS

To flavour spirits, simply add the flavouring of your choice, for example fruit, nuts, peel, chillis, garlic, chocolate or herbs and leave to stand. Vodka is the most widely used base spirit for infusion and since it is light in character allows the flavours to show themselves fully. That said, gin is wonderful (think sloe and damson) as is tequila (chilli, even lemon) and overproof rum. You can even use a moscato grappa for a walnut-based infusion and it works well. If you can find high-strength Polish Pure Spirit use it; the high alcohol level means extraction is quicker. Dilute the result with standard strength vodka. Overproof rum works on the same principle.

You can use sweet or savoury ingredients as flavourings. Do not fall into the trap of using only sweet ingredients: chocolate vodka, for example, is fun the first time you try it, but the novelty soon wears off. Savoury/fresh fruit infusions tend to be more versatile and interesting.

THE COCKTAILS

Tim
McStraw

SUGGESTED LISTENING:
Tim McGraw

A dash of grenadine adds some delightful sweetness to the sourness of the whiskey, providing the perfect duet and reflecting Taylor's age, sweet 16, when she released this debut single. The song, named after the renowned country artist she admired, was an immediate hit and poignantly asks an ex-boyfriend to remember her every time he hears her favourite song. We're pretty sure that the McStraw will become a firm favourite too.

INGREDIENTS

2 oz. (60 ml/4 tbsp.) bourbon
1 oz. (30 ml/2 tbsp.) fresh lemon
    juice
½ oz. (15 ml/1 tbsp.) gomme syrup
dash grenadine

METHOD

Shake the ingredients, then strain
    into an ice-filled old-fashioned
    glass.
Add a straw to serve.

Lemon Drop on My Guitar

SUGGESTED LISTENING:
Teardrops on My Guitar

Oh, the pain of unrequited love! This beautiful second single recalls feelings for a high school classmate who was so oblivious to her affection that he would casually talk to her about another girl he had a crush on and she pretended to think it endearing. The bitter-sweet memory of adolescent love is mirrored in this lemony, sweet mix.

INGREDIENTS
1 lemon wedge
1 tsp. sugar
1 oz. (30 ml/2 tbsp.) vodka

METHOD
Dip the lemon wedge in the sugar and pour the vodka into a shot glass.
Drink the vodka first, then suck the lemon.

Should've Said Prosecco

As bubbly as Taylor herself, Prosecco's light, fun taste always puts a smile on the face. If you have ever been upset and angry about a cheating ex, as Taylor was in this song, then the slightly bitter taste here is eased by the citrus notes and the effervescence of the Prosecco or Champagne. One sip will instantly have you feeling better.

INGREDIENTS
1 oz. (30 ml/2 tbsp.) Campari
½ oz. (15 ml/1 tbsp.) sweet
    vermouth
Champagne or Prosecco

METHOD
Shake the ingredients, then
    pour into a champagne flute.
Fill up with Champagne or
    Prosecco and serve.

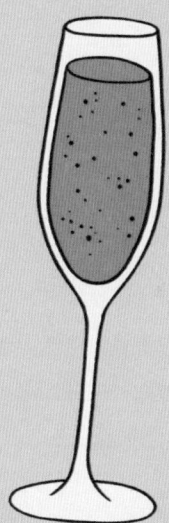

Whisky Sour Song

SUGGESTED LISTENING:
Our Song

There's sweet and sour in all of our lives, right? The earthy whisky and the sweetness of the syrup are perfect partners in this cocktail, just like the young couple in 'Our Song', written by Taylor for a high school talent show. In this song, the loved-up pair create their own love song via the sounds of everyday things in their lives – the closing of a screen door and tapping on a window – which provide the soundtrack to their relationship.

INGREDIENTS

2 oz. (60 ml/4 tbsp.) whisky
1 oz. (30 ml/2 tbsp.) fresh
    lemon juice
½ oz. (15 ml/1 tbsp.)
    gomme syrup

METHOD

Shake the whisky, lemon juice
    and syrup, then pour into
    an old-fashioned glass
    and serve.

Paloma Me When I'm With You

SUGGESTED LISTENING:

I'm Only Me When I'm With You

Taylor is famous for her girl squad and is never more comfortable than when she is surrounded by her besties. A Margarita is the cocktail equivalent of a bff but if you want to try a new pal, cosy up with a Paloma, which shares the same tequila and lime but with grapefruit to give it a pleasing, citrusy sharpness.

INGREDIENTS
2 oz. (60 ml/4 tbsp.) tequila
2 oz. (60 ml/4 tbsp.) grapefruit juice
1 oz. (30 ml/2 tbsp.) agave syrup
juice of 1 lime
soda water
slice of grapefruit to garnish

METHOD
Shake all of the ingredients,
    except the soda water, in a
    shaker with ice.
Strain into a salt-rimmed
    margarita glass.
Top with the soda water and garnish
    with the grapefruit slice and serve.

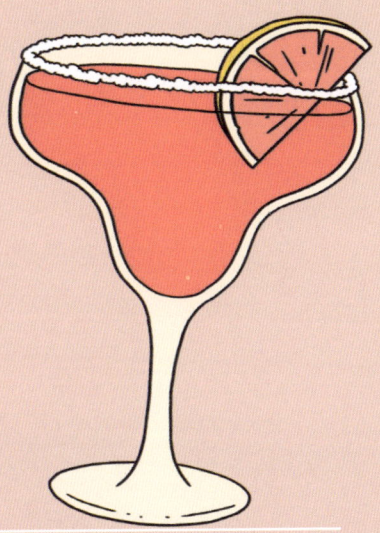

Fiftini

SUGGESTED LISTENING:
Fifteen

When someone says they love you at 15, you totally believe it, and Taylor wrote this song about Abigail, her best friend at school, who had her heart broken when a boy dumped her. The pair clicked because they both felt like outsiders at school, but there's nothing wrong with being different. Stand out in a crowd with this classy dry concoction, and savour a touch of spice from Noilly Prat vermouth.

INGREDIENTS
½ oz. (15 ml/1tsp.) Noilly Prat vermouth
3 oz. (90 ml/6 tbsp.) chilled dry gin
olive or twist of lemon to garnish

METHOD
Place the vermouth in shaker with ice. Shake and strain away the excess. Add the gin. Stir and strain into a pre-chilled cocktail glass.
Add the olive or lemon twist. Serve. You can vary the amount of vermouth to taste, but the principle remains the same.

White Russian Horse

White Horse

Sweet, creamy, and rich – this is effectively a yummy boozy milkshake! The Kahlúa coffee liqueur, with a dollop of cream, makes it smooth like velvet. Stare into the glass at the swirling, dramatic depths, and imagine the sunset that fairytale fan Taylor imagined riding off into, on a white horse, with her Prince Charming.

INGREDIENTS
1 oz. (30 ml/2 tbsp.) vodka
1 oz. (30 ml/2 tbsp.) Kahlúa
1 oz. (30 ml/2 tbsp.) heavy
    (double) cream

METHOD
Shake the ingredients, then strain
    into a martini glass and serve.
Alternatively, layer the
    ingredients in an ice-filled
    old-fashioned glass.

You Be-long Island Iced Tea With Me

With four spirits fighting for taste, this is not for the fainthearted. It's named for having the same colour as iced tea but, make no mistake, it packs an alcoholic punch. Taylor may have been writing about falling for a boy whose girlfriend doesn't appreciate him, but you will definitely appreciate this classic drink.

INGREDIENTS
juice of 1 lime
½ oz. (15 ml/1 tbsp.) light rum
½ oz. (15 ml/1 tbsp.) vodka
½ oz. (15 ml/1 tbsp.) gin
½ oz. (15 ml/1 tbsp.) tequila
½ oz. (15 ml/1 tbsp.) triple sec
cola

METHOD
Squeeze the lime into a
    highball glass, then add ice
    cubes and the spirits and
    triple sec.
Stir and fill up with cola. Serve
    with straws.

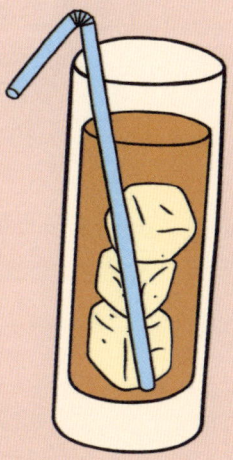

Mr.
Perfectly
Wine

SUGGESTED LISTENING:
Mr. Perfectly Fine

Wow is this bitter! And we're talking both the drink and the song. The Campari and the lemon provide a tartness that reflects this caustic and sarcastic song about a former flame who promised a life together but then cold-heartedly walked out when he got bored. The tongue-twisting word play was much admired, just like this tantalizing tipple.

INGREDIENTS
¾ oz. (22 ml/1½ tbsp.) fresh lemon
   juice
¼ oz. (8 ml/½ tbsp.) Campari
¾ oz. (22 ml/1½ tbsp.) Cordial
   Campari
Champagne

METHOD
Shake the lemon juice and both
   Camparis, then strain into a
   champagne flute.
Fill with Champagne, stir and
   serve.

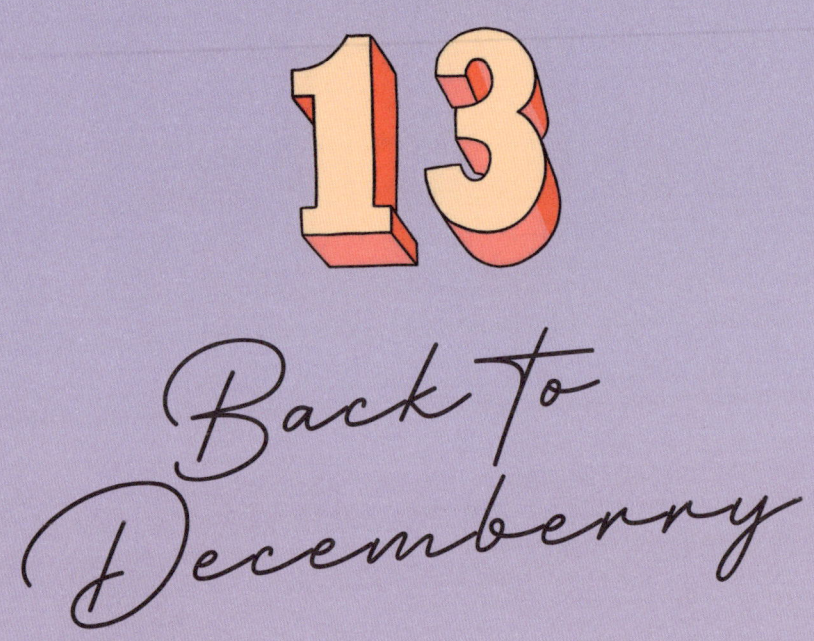

13

Back to Decemberry

A sweet one for sweethearts. This power ballad from her third album was a departure from diss songs about her exes, with Taylor apologizing to a former love for having hurt him and realizing she had made a mistake. This punch is a fruity treat that's perfect for two to share, ideal for if the reconciliation goes well.

INGREDIENTS

1 tbsp. brown sugar
2 small limes, diced
few raspberries
few blueberries
6 strawberries, hulled and diced
2 oz. (60 ml/4 tbsp.) cachaça

METHOD

Add the sugar and the pieces of lime to the bottom of a small bowl. Muddle the lime, releasing the juices, then add the berries.
Muddle some more. Place a scoop of this mixture into an old-fashioned glass.
Add the cachaça and crushed ice and stir. Serve with a stirrer and a straw.

Dear John Collins

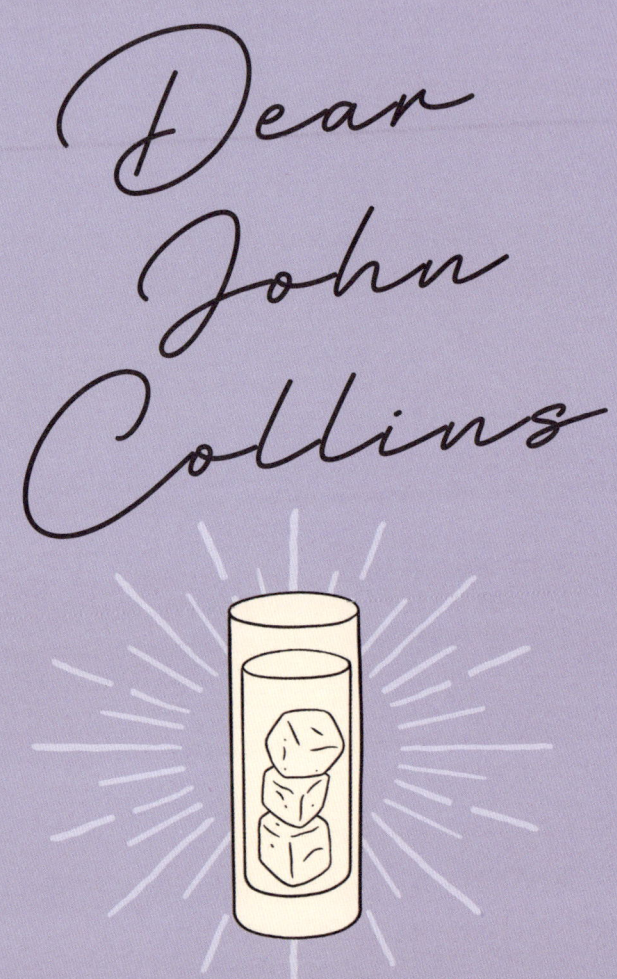

SUGGESTED LISTENING:
Dear John

Referencing the traditional 'Dear John' letter written to a man when ending a relationship, this powerful ballad tells of a 19-year-old's relationship with an older, controlling man. It is reflected here with what might be described as a 'grown-up lemonade', the classic Tom Collins cocktail. If a Gin and Soda or Tonic is a tad astringent for you, try this refreshing and zesty alternative with sugar to sweeten.

INGREDIENTS
2 oz. (60 ml/4 tbsp.) gin
1 oz. (30 ml/2 tbsp.) fresh lemon juice
1 tsp. superfine (caster) sugar
dash Angostura bitters (optional)
soda water

METHOD
Place the first four ingredients
    in an ice-filled highball glass,
    then stir to mix.
Fill up with soda water.
Stir gently and serve.

Bitter Than Revenge

This has a sharp bite, like Taylor's caustic attack on a love rival in this song that she memorably included on the set list of her 2011–2012 Speak Now World Tour. Looking fabulous as ever, she appeared in a sparkly red dress, singing from a bridge and pretend-fighting with a dancer. Thankfully, with the drink, there is a mellow undertone, so it goes down easier than the song would have for the scorned lover.

INGREDIENTS

1 oz. (30 ml/2 tbsp.) Campari
1 oz. (30 ml/2 tbsp.) tequila
½ oz. (15 ml/1 tbsp.)
    Cointreau
1 egg white

METHOD

 Shake the ingredients, then
    strain into a martini glass
    and serve.

SHAKE OF GRACE

SUGGESTED LISTENING:
State of Grace

Jangling guitars with a heavy, rhythmic drum beat, 'State of Grace' took Taylor into rock territory while describing those overwhelming feelings that batter the senses at the first signs of love. But this pleasingly fruity and tart drink will not have your head pounding. Just like the song there's an element of grace. And not only does it taste divine, it looks like a sunset in a glass!

INGREDIENTS

1 oz. (30 ml/2 tbsp.) apricot brandy
1 oz. (30 ml/2 tbsp.) sloe gin
1 oz. (30 ml/2 tbsp.) fresh lemon juice

METHOD

Shake the ingredients, then strain into a martini glass and serve.

RED
RASPBERRY
MARTINI

SUGGESTED LISTENING:
Red

Vibrant red in colour and full of berry flavour, this cocktail is every bit as intense as the title song of Taylor's fourth album *Red*. Taylor describes the swirl of complex and conflicting feelings as the colours of the rainbow with love coming out on top as red. The power of this emotion is reflected in the deep tone of this delicious drink as the crème de framboise raspberry liqueur packs a flavoursome punch.

INGREDIENTS
10 raspberries
2 oz. (60 ml/4 tbsp.) vodka
1 oz. (30 ml/2 tbsp.) crème de framboise

METHOD
Muddle the raspberries in a shaker.
Add the vodka and crème de framboise.
Shake, then strain into a martini glass
and serve.

I KNEW
YOU WERE
DOUBLE

SUGGESTED LISTENING:
I Knew You Were Trouble

The dynamic duo of the two fruity but contrasting vodkas might have you seeing double if you have too many. So go easy and savour the various tastes, heightened by the spicy and aromatic Angostura bitters. The punchy taste will smooth away any frustration of helplessly falling in love with the wrong person as Taylor explores in her hit song 'I Knew You Were Trouble'.

INGREDIENTS
1 oz. (30 ml/2 tbsp.) lemon vodka
1 oz. (30 ml/2 tbsp.) blackcurrant vodka
4 dashes Angostura bitters
1 oz. (30 ml/2 tbsp.) apple juice

METHOD
Shake the ingredients, then strain into a
    martini glass and serve.

WE ARE
NEVER EVER
GETTING
BACK TEQUILA

SUGGESTED LISTENING:

We Are Never Ever Getting Back Together

Ugh. Relationships can be the worst. Especially when they're on-off-on again. But fear not, help is at hand in the shape of our old friend, tequila! Name-checked by Taylor herself in 'You Need To Calm Down', when you are getting sick of the latest ups and downs of a problematic romance, pour out this oh-so-simple blend of tequila and fruit juices and let your mind drift away to a beautiful Mexican town.

INGREDIENTS
2 oz. (60 ml/4 tbsp.) tequila
dash triple sec
4 oz. (120 ml/8 tbsp.) cranberry
   juice
$1/3$ oz. (10 ml/$2/3$ tbsp.) pineapple
   juice
$1/3$ oz. (10 ml/$2/3$ tbsp.) fresh orange
   juice

METHOD
Pour the first three ingredients into
   an ice-filled highball glass.
Stir, then add the pineapple and
   orange juices.
Stir, then serve with a stirrer.

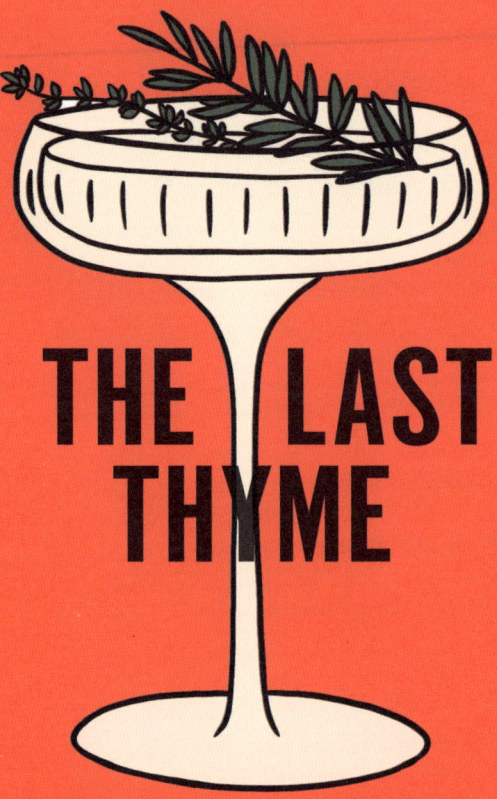

THE LAST THYME

Simon & Garfunkel sang about parsley, sage, rosemary and thyme in the classic 'Scarborough Fair'. Well, here they are with a splash of Plymouth gin, which adds peppery and floral notes, plus the spicy Chambéry vermouth, to create a cocktail packed with a variety of flavours. The song might be about giving a partner just one more chance but, trust us, this won't be the last time you drink this!

INGREDIENTS
2 fresh sage leaves
sprig of flat-leaf parsley
¼ oz. (8 ml/½ tbsp.) Chambéry
2 oz. (60 ml/4 tbsp.) Plymouth gin
sprig of rosemary to garnish
sprig of thyme to garnish

METHOD
Muddle the sage, parsley and Chambéry
    in a shaker. Add the gin.
Shake, then strain into a cocktail glass.
Garnish with rosemary and
    thyme leaves and serve.

HOLY GROUNDS

SUGGESTED LISTENING:
Holy Ground

Give a coffee break some pizzazz! Rich and creamy with a kick, it is similar to an Irish Coffee, which uses Irish whiskey instead of bourbon and adds a bit of depth. One sip provides an instant adrenalin hit, putting a smile on your face like the memory of a good moment in a failed relationship. Pleasure truly can be found in murky depths!

INGREDIENTS
1 oz. (30 ml/2 tbsp.) bourbon
6 oz. (180 ml/12 tbsp.) hot black coffee
2 tsp. raw (Demerara) sugar
heavy (double) cream

METHOD
Pour the bourbon and black coffee into a liqueur coffee glass, then add the sugar.
Float the cream on top and serve.

STARLIGHT
SPRITZ

SUGGESTED LISTENING:
Starlight

This screams old-school romance with the punchy white rum and blackberry overload from the fruit and liquor. The Champagne mirrors the frivolous, bubbly fun of teenagers in love, with dancing and heady exciting times when no one else matters but each other. Taylor was inspired to write the song after coming across a photo of Bobby and Ethel Kennedy dancing when they were teenagers.

INGREDIENTS
4 blackberries
dash gomme syrup
$^1/_3$ oz. (10 ml/$^2/_3$ tbsp.) crème de mure
1 oz. (30 ml/2 tbsp.) white rum
half a slice of orange
Champagne

METHOD
Muddle the berries with the gomme and
    crème de mure in a shaker.
Add the rum. Squeeze the slice of orange
    over it and add ice cubes.
Shake and strain into a champagne flute.
    Fill with Champagne. Stir and serve.

BE-GIN AGAIN

SUGGESTED LISTENING:
Begin Again

True love seldom comes easily, but good things come to those who wait and have the strength to try again. Like this fruit cocktail, which you won't mind trying again and again! The unmistakable flavour of lychee lifts it beyond expectations with the peach slice, as garnish, giving a warming, mouth-watering side show to the main attraction.

INGREDIENTS
1 oz. (30 ml/2 tbsp.) gin
$^2/_3$ oz. (20 ml/$1^1/_3$ tbsp.) lychee liqueur
$^2/_3$ oz. (20 ml/$1^1/_3$ tbsp.) pineapple liqueur
$^2/_3$ oz. (20 ml/$1^1/_3$ tbsp.) fresh peach purée
peach slice to garnish

METHOD
Shake the ingredients, strain into a cocktail glass, add the peach slice and serve.

THE MOMENT I BLUE

Oh, what a fun drink this is. Sapphire blue, the perfect company if you are on a beach or just dreaming of one. Its vibrant, dramatic colour is a real crowd pleaser at a party, too, and it's as refreshing as a plunge into the ocean. Taylor was feeling blue, too, when she wrote about a boyfriend not turning up at 21st birthday party and her feeling publicly 'stood up'.

INGREDIENTS
8 fresh blueberries
2 oz. (60 ml/4 tbsp.) vodka
$^1/_3$ oz. (10 ml/$^2/_3$ tbsp.) blue Curaçao
$^1/_3$ oz. (10 ml/$^2/_3$ tbsp.) fresh lemon juice

METHOD
Muddle the blueberries in the bottom
    of a shaker.
Add the remaining ingredients.
Shake, then strain into a cocktail glass
    and serve.

I BET YOU DRINK ABOUT ME

SUGGESTED LISTENING:
I Bet You Think About Me

This delicious, golden orange, spicy-sweet cocktail is one you'll be thinking about for a long time after you've tasted it. It's as unforgettable as Taylor imagines she is to her ex (rumoured to be Jake Gyllenhaal) when she teases him in song about leaving her because he felt his wealthy background was too contrasting from hers. You can't buy class, but this mix is bursting with it.

INGREDIENTS
1 oz. (30 ml/2 tbsp.) vodka
1 oz. (30 ml/2 tbsp.) Mandarine
  Napoléon
1 oz. (30 ml/2 tbsp.) mandarin juice
2 dashes Angostura bitters

METHOD
Shake the ingredients, then strain
  into a cocktail glass and serve.

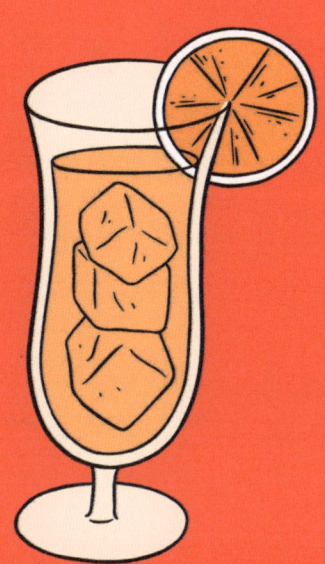

ALL TOO WELL (10-MINT JULEP VERSION)

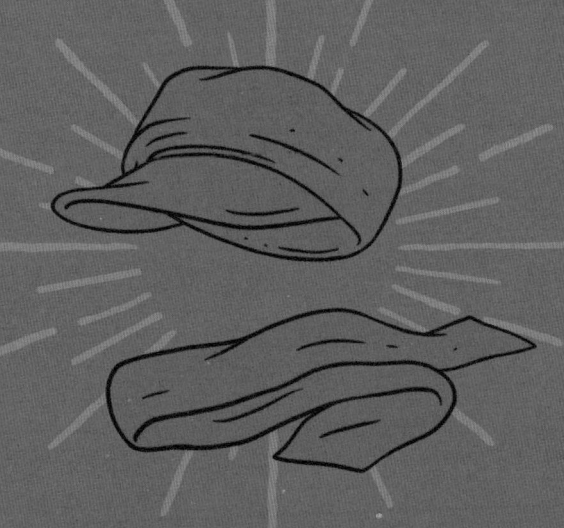

SUGGESTED LISTENING:
All Too Well (10 Minute Version)

This is summer in a glass. Closely identified with America's Deep South and famously served at the Kentucky Derby, the Mint Julep is wonderfully simple to make and won't take 10 minutes like the extended version of Taylor's song about a failed relationship. But that is about the right amount of time it should take to drink it before the ice melts. There's nothing quite like it on a hot day.

INGREDIENTS
finely crushed ice
3 oz. (90 ml/6 tbsp.) bourbon
1 oz. (30 ml/2 tbsp.) simple syrup
6 sprigs of mint

METHOD
Fill a highball glass two-thirds full
    with crushed ice.
Add the bourbon and syrup. Stir.
Pack the glass with more ice so it
    domes over the top.
Garnish with the mint and insert
    straws. Let stand until a thin layer of
    frost forms on the glass, then serve.

FRENCH 89

Who doesn't want to appear fresh, sharp and sophisticated? The French 89 does exactly this, effervescent with a pleasant citrus tartness and hint of sweetness from the syrup.

Our take on the classic French 75 classic cocktail, this version is named after Taylor's year of birth and her record-breaking 1989 album, symbolizing her rebirth as an artist moving from Nashville to Manhattan and from country to pop. This drink is the perfect way to celebrate and toast her success.

INGREDIENTS
¾ oz. (22 ml/1½ tbsp.) gin
¼ oz. (8 ml/½ tbsp.) fresh
    lemon juice
dash gomme syrup
dash grenadine
Champagne

METHOD
Shake the first four ingredients,
    then strain into a champagne
    flute, fill with Champagne
    and serve.

WELCOME TO MANHATTAN

SUGGESTED LISTENING:
Welcome to New York

Rich and warm with a light sweetness is a description that fits our muse as well as this classic drink. The lyrics to this song explore her love for New York and a lighter attitude towards past heartbreaks. Similarly, the sweet vermouth in the internationally popular Manhattan cocktail softens the spirit, reducing the heat. There's a dash of bitter from the Angostura but it's the cherry that adds the fun.

INGREDIENTS

2 oz. (60 ml/4 tbsp.)
  rye whiskey
1 oz. (30 ml/2 tbsp.)
  sweet vermouth
3 dashes Angostura
drop of maraschino juice
maraschino cherry

METHOD

Stir the first four ingredients in a mixing glass, then strain into cocktail glass.
Drop the cherry in the glass and serve.

OLD STYLE

SUGGESTED LISTENING:
Style

In the catchy 'Style', Taylor sings about an on-and-off-again relationship between two lovers who are reuniting, just like our old friends bourbon and Angostura! Many Swifties believe the song is about Harry Styles, who she was dating just before making 1989. This Taylor Swift take on the traditional whiskey Old Fashioned cocktail is full of style, lightly sweetened with sugar and aromatized with bitters. Some things are worth coming back to, again and again.

INGREDIENTS
3 dashes Angostura bitters
1 sugar cube
3 oz. (90 ml/6 tbsp.) bourbon
slice of orange
maraschino cherry to garnish

METHOD
Put the bitters, sugar cube and a dash of the bourbon into an old-fashioned glass and muddle.

Add two ice cubes and 2 tablespoons of the bourbon and stir.

Squeeze some of the juice from the orange slice into the glass, then add two more ice cubes and 2 more tablespoons of the bourbon and stir again.

Finally, add two more ice cubes and the remaining bourbon. Garnish with the orange slice and the cherry.

ALL YOU HAD TO DO WAS SHAKE

This colourful, fruity, rum-laced drink packs enough punch to transport you to sunny Jamaica. You can get in the party mood when you are making it because this one needs a lot of shakin' going on. So, get in the groove and dance away any frustration, just as Taylor sings about in this song lamenting the end of a relationship.

INGREDIENTS
1 slice pineapple
1 tsp. granulated sugar
2 oz. (60 ml/4 tbsp.) Jamaican rum
juice of 1 lime
dash grenadine

METHOD
Sprinkle a slice of pineapple with the sugar. Crush with a muddler in the shaker base, then add the rum, lime juice, grenadine and some crushed ice.
Shake long and vigorously, then strain into a cocktail glass and serve.

I WHISKEY YOU WOULD

SUGGESTED LISTENING:
I Wish You Would

We all have regrets when we make the wrong decisions and wish we hadn't said something or acted in a certain way. But being bold is to be admired. Take this beautiful amber-hued drink, for example, with a robust nose of grain, fruit and herbs. A true classic Irish cocktail that dates back over 100 years, the green Chartreuse adds a kick but all the flavours come together in perfect harmony.

INGREDIENTS
1 oz. (30 ml/2 tbsp.) Irish whiskey
¾ oz. (22 ml/1½ tbsp.) dry vermouth
¼ oz. (8 ml/½ tbsp.) green Chartreuse

METHOD
Shake the ingredients, then strain into an old fashioned glass and serve.

BAD
BLOODY MARY

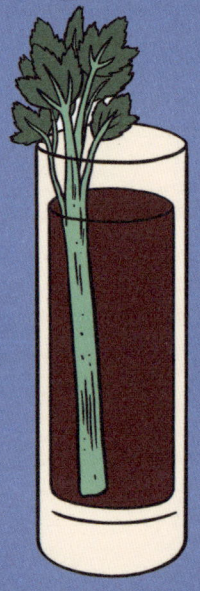

SUGGESTED LISTENING:
Bad Blood

One of the world's best-known cocktails, the Bloody Mary is a traditional hangover cure prized for its ability to jumpstart the groggiest of heads. The spicy tomato kick with zesty citrus fruit and earthy undertone make it slip down easily. 'Bad Blood' explores betrayal by a close friend, but there's nothing bad about this delicious cocktail!

INGREDIENTS
2 oz. (60 ml/4 tbsp.) vodka
6 oz. (180 ml/12 tbsp.) tomato juice
2 dashes Worcestershire sauce
pinch black pepper
pinch celery salt
½ oz. (15 ml/1 tbsp.) fresh lemon juice
Tabasco sauce (to taste)

METHOD
Pour the vodka over ice in a highball glass.
  Combine the other ingredients in a jug,
    then add the mix to the vodka.
(A celery stick is optional!)

HOW YOU GET THE GIMLET

SUGGESTED LISTENING:
How You Get the Girl

Light and refreshing, a bit like Taylor's advice to
a male pal about the best way to go about getting
a girlfriend back. This effortlessly tangy tipple
needs no help winning hearts with ease. The gimlet
cocktail is a simple but a classic combination and
the ingredients are easy to find anywhere. Perfect
to enjoy with friends if they drop in unannounced to
seek advice on their own love lives.

INGREDIENTS
2 oz. (60 ml/4 tbsp.) gin or vodka
1 oz. (30 ml/2 tbsp.) lime cordial
wedge of lime to garnish

METHOD
Pour the spirit and lime cordial over ice
    cubes in a cocktail glass, garnish with the
    lime wedge and serve.

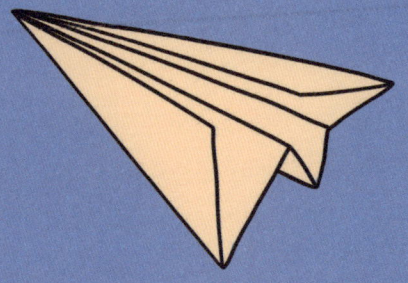

NEW
RUM-ANTICS

Feeling down? Then lift your spirits with this rich and fruity tastebud tingler. Shrub is a fruit-infused vinegar syrup and, mixed with rum and soda, it makes for a bracing drink. It's a taste of history, too, dating back to 17th-century England and favoured by colonial Americans when vinegar was used to preserve berries and other fruits. In 'New Romantics', Taylor wrote about reigniting her hopes after heartbreak and a sip of this cocktail will certainly restore your faith in romance.

INGREDIENTS
2 oz. (60 ml/4 tbsp.) dark rum
1 oz. (30 ml/2 tbsp.) shrub (fruit
 and herb syrup)
1 oz. (30 ml/2 tbsp.) soda water

METHOD
Fill wine glass two-thirds with ice.
Add the rum, shrub and soda water.
Stir lightly and serve.

FLAMINGO PINK GIN

SUGGESTED LISTENING:
"Slut!"

This simple pink gin has some spicy bitterness from the Angostura with notes of cloves and cinnamon to perk you up and help you strut your stuff whenever you want to flaunt it. As Taylor says in this song in defiance to slut-shamers, just dress up and take centre stage and what better way to do so than with this gorgeous pink cocktail?

INGREDIENTS
2 dashes Angostura bitters
4 oz. (120 ml/8 tbsp.) gin

METHOD
Coat a chilled cocktail glass with the Angostura bitters.
Discard the excess, fill up with the gin and serve.

NOW THAT WE DON'T TONIC

SUGGESTED LISTENING:
Now That We Don't Talk

There is no better partnership than the timeless Gin and Tonic, a quintessential English drink (and we know Taylor likes an Englishman) dating back to the British Empire when tonic was added to officers' gin as an effective antidote to malaria. Unlike the ultimate pairing of Gin and Tonic here, 'Now That We Don't Talk' bemoans the ending of a relationship – sounds like Taylor needs a cocktail to soothe her spirits!

INGREDIENTS
2 oz. (60 ml/4 tbsp.) gin
4–6oz. (120 ml/8 tbsp.–180 ml/12 tbsp.)
    tonic (to taste)
wedge of lime to garnish

METHOD
Fill a highball glass or gin goblet with ice.
Add the gin and the tonic, to taste.
Garnish with the lime wedge and serve.

SUBOURBON LEGENDS

SUGGESTED LISTENING:
Suburban Legends

Perfect for star-crossed lovers everywhere, like in this song which follows the weaving narrative of a long-term relationship which may lead to a doomed climax but there will be fun and good times along the way. An enticing mix of sweet and sour with a zingy vibe and delicious orange flavour from the Cointreau.

INGREDIENTS
1 oz. (30 ml/2 tbsp.) Cointreau
1 oz. (30 ml/2 tbsp.) bourbon
1 oz. (30 ml/2 tbsp.) dry vermouth
slice of orange to garnish

METHOD
Pour the ingredients into an old-fashioned glass and stir, then garnish with the orange slice and serve.

FIZZ IT OVER NOW?

The confusion of the aftermath of a break-up, rumoured to be with Harry Styles, has Taylor in anxious mode. Clearly, she is in need of this relaxing, peachy-smooth twist on the famous Bellini. Adding mango and peach purée, peach brandy and a dash of lemon creates a wonderful fruity and tangy balance with the Bellini elegance and sophistication. It can be enjoyed at any time of the day!

INGREDIENTS
6 oz. (180 ml/12 tbsp.) fresh white
    peach purée
dash peach brandy
2 oz. (60 ml/4 tbsp.) mango purée
Prosecco

METHOD
Stir peach purée and brandy in a
    champagne flute.
Add the mango purée, fill up with
    the Prosecco, stir and serve.

sloe it goes

Lose yourself in this sweet indulgence, just as Taylor describes the all-consuming emotion of a love affair. The raspberry liqueur with the tang of the sloe gin and tartness of the dry vermouth is a match made in heaven. Ideal for two to share, or for one who's lost in dreams of love.

INGREDIENTS

1 oz. (30 ml/2 tbsp.) sloe gin

1 oz. (30 ml/2 tbsp.) dry
   vermouth

½ oz. (15 ml/1 tbsp.) crème de
   framboise

maraschino cherry to garnish

METHOD

Pour the ingredients into
a cocktail glass, then stir.
Garnish with the cherry
and serve.

look what you made me brew

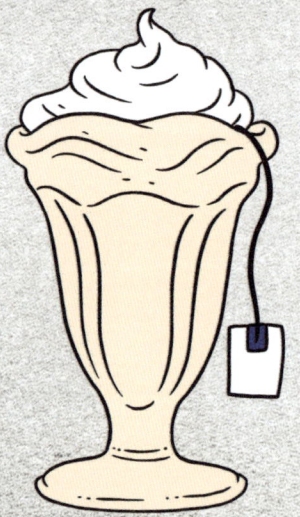

SUGGESTED LISTENING:
Look What You Made Me Do

There is powerful imagery in the video for this song about vengeance but, while revenge is best served cold, this warm, creamy drink is perfect to take the edge off any resentment about a past love. Get yourself an ornate parfait glass, the sort that is often used to serve a milkshake and follow the oh-so-easy recipe below. It makes for the ideal nightcap, with a sweet, almondy taste, warming you through, right down to your toes!

INGREDIENTS

6 oz. (180 ml/12 tbsp.) hot tea
2 oz. (60 ml/4 tbsp.) amaretto
whipped cream for topping

METHOD

Place a spoon in a parfait glass, then pour in the hot tea. (The spoon prevents the glass from cracking.)

Add the amaretto, without stirring, and top off with the whipped cream and serve.

getaway
sidecar

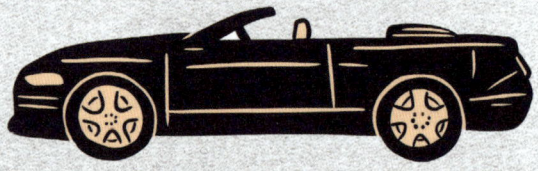

SUGGESTED LISTENING:

Getaway Car

This is all about getting the balance right. And we are sure you will agree that it does with the rich oomph of cognac, the subtle sweetness from the Cointreau, the shot of orange and sharpness of the lemon juice. Taylor wanted to drive away from a relationship and this concoction, based on a Sidecar cocktail, is pure escapism. The original was said to have been invented in Paris during the First World War by a man who used to arrive at Harry's New York Bar in a chauffeur-driven motorcycle sidecar.

INGREDIENTS
1 oz. (30 ml/2 tbsp.) cognac
²/₃ oz. (20 ml/1¹/₃ tbsp.)
   Cointreau
²/₃ oz. (20 ml/1¹/₃ tbsp.) fresh
   lemon juice

METHOD
Shake the ingredients, then
   strain into a cocktail glass
   and serve.

king of my bar cart

SUGGESTED LISTENING:
King of My Heart

Sometimes you feel done with relationships and just want to be on your own and then, pow! Somebody unexpectedly enters your life. That's just how this beautiful orange-coloured summer drink feels, with its fun blend of citrus, rich mandarin liqueur, sweet zing of limoncello, livener of gin and the bittersweet notes of the Aperol. Suddenly you are sitting up and taking notice!

INGREDIENTS
1 oz. (30 ml/2 tbsp.) gin
$^2/_3$ oz. (20 ml/1$^1/_3$ tbsp.) Aperol
½ oz. (15 ml/1 tbsp.) limoncello
½ oz. (15 ml/1 tbsp.) mandarin
    liqueur
$^2/_3$ oz. (20 ml/1$^1/_3$ tbsp.) fresh
    orange juice
lime spiral to garnish

METHOD
Shake the ingredients, then strain
    into a cocktail glass.
Add the lime spiral and serve.

this is why we can't have nice gins

The bitter orange adds complexity to this mix of daring ingredients which explores conflict in friendships, rumoured to be about Taylor's difficult relationship with Kanye West. However, sweetness from the syrup and raspberries shows that even the greatest falling out can be overcome, and what better way to make reparations than sharing this delicious cocktail?

INGREDIENTS
2 oz. (60 ml/4 tbsp.) gin
1 oz. (30 ml/2 tbsp.) Cointreau
dash gomme syrup
dash Peychaud's bitters
9 raspberries, 3 to garnish

METHOD
Shake the ingredients, then strain
    into a cocktail glass.
Add 3 raspberries on a cocktail
    stick across the glass and serve.

Cruel Slammer

SUGGESTED LISTENING:
Cruel Summer

You've got to trust in this one... Yes, the ingredients look like they have been thrown together by without any thought but the result is surprising. It's sweet, fruity and nutty but with an alcoholic punch and a luxurious orange glow in appearance. Deep, complex but rewarding. Like a sunset during an intense summer romance with multi-layered emotions.

INGREDIENTS
1 oz. (30 ml/2 tbsp.) amaretto
1 oz. (30 ml/2 tbsp.)
    Southern Comfort
1 oz. (30 ml/2 tbsp.) sloe gin
dash fresh lemon juice

METHOD
Stir the amaretto, Southern Comfort
    and sloe gin in a mixing glass, then
    strain into a shot glass.
Add the lemon juice and serve.

Miss American Fizz & the Heartbreak Prince

This Taylor version of the American Fizz cocktail is a heady mix of deep sweetness and effervescence. Taylor wrote this intriguing protest song a few months after the 2018 US mid-term elections, cleverly likening the political scene to homecoming queens and marching bands to convey her confusion and angst at the American political climate. There's a happy ending though as she finds her prince to help her get through it, just like this cocktail will soothe you.

INGREDIENTS
1 oz. (30 ml/2 tbsp.) dark rum
1 oz. (30 ml/2 tbsp.) banana purée
1 oz. (30 ml/2 tbsp.) pineapple juice
Champagne

METHOD
Shake the ingredients, except the
    Champagne.
Strain into a champagne flute.
Fill with Champagne, stir and serve.

Death by a Thousand Shots

SUGGESTED LISTENING:
Death by a Thousand Cuts

Oh, what fun this is and it looks spectacular, as long as you have a steady hand! By carefully layering the almond-flavoured crème de noix, Galliano's golden vanilla and the striking green Midori with its burst of melon, you can create a flavour sensation! Taylor's song was inspired by watching the rom com *Someone Great* on Netflix comparing the pain of a break-up to a slow, painful death. Sounds like this drink may help!

INGREDIENTS

1 oz. (30 ml/2 tbsp.) crème de noix
1 oz. (30 ml/2 tbsp.) Galliano
1 oz. (30 ml/2 tbsp.) Midori

METHOD

In a shot glass, layer each of the
  ingredients in turn and serve.

London Gin Boy

SUGGESTED LISTENING:
London Boy

It's always Martini thyme, right? And when there's a fresh herbal touch with the distinctive taste of Chartreuse, then it's a capital idea. The lyrics here reference Tay's time in London with her former partner, English actor Joe Alwyn. It has a memorable spoken-word intro by another Londoner Idris Elba. And of course, the cocktail features London gin, making this the perfect accompaniment to the song celebrating this city.

INGREDIENTS
3 oz. (90 ml/6 tbsp.) London gin
¾ oz. (22 ml/1½ tbsp.)
   green Chartreuse
sprig of thyme to garnish

METHOD
Stir the gin and Chartreuse
   in a mixing glass.
Strain into a martini glass,
   garnish with the thyme
   and serve.

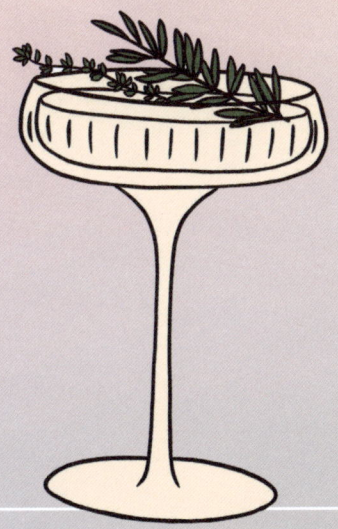

You Need Amaret-to Calm Down

SUGGESTED LISTENING:
You Need to Calm Down

A creamy vodka-based drink which is almost as much fun as the time celebrities such as Katy Perry, Laverne Cox, RuPaul and Ryan Reynolds were having in the memorable video for this song which kicks back at internet trolls and homophobes. Set in a rainbow-hued trailer park and loudly voicing her support for the LGBTQ+ community, it culminates in a food fight with Taylor dressed as takeaway fries meeting her perfect partner, Katy Perry as a burger!

INGREDIENTS
1 oz. (30 ml/2 tbsp.) vodka
²/₃ oz. (20 ml/1¹/₃ tbsp.) amaretto
²/₃ oz. (20 ml/1¹/₃ tbsp.) coconut
    cream

METHOD
Shake the ingredients, then strain
    into a martini glass and serve.

ME!jito

A cocktail born in Havana, Cuba, the Mojito is – much like the song that has inspired this version – light and sweet with a bright zing to it. A pure celebration of individualism and empowerment, 'ME!' is the perfect song to soundtrack such a unique drink. And in the spirit of collaboration that led Taylor to duet with Panic! At The Disco's Brandon Urie, this is one to scale up, pour out and share with friends.

INGREDIENTS
fresh mint leaves
1 tsp. gomme syrup
half a lime
2 oz. (60 ml/4 tbsp.)
    white rum
soda water
sprig of mint to garnish

METHOD
In a highball glass, muddle the
    mint leaves and syrup.
Squeeze lime juice into the glass
    and add the lime half.
Add the rum and ice and stir.
Add soda water, stir briefly, garnish
    with the mint sprig and serve.

Negroni the Young

PAIR WITH:
Only the Young

An outtake from *Lover*, 'Only the Young' was featured in the must-watch documentary *Miss Americana*, which follows Taylor's writing process as she brings the song to life from scratch. You can bring your own creation to life with this cocktail inspired by the song, a bitter and tart Italian classic that mixes equal parts Campari and sweet vermouth into a delicious drink with an on-brand red hue.

INGREDIENTS
1½ oz. (45 ml/3 tbsp.) gin
1½ oz. (45 ml/3 tbsp.) Campari
1½ oz. (45 ml/3 tbsp.) sweet vermouth
soda water (optional)
slice of orange to garnish

METHOD
Shake the ingredients, then pour over ice in a highball glass. Fill with soda water, add the garnish and serve.

cardi-rita

SUGGESTED LISTENING:
cardigan

The classic Margarita. Invigorating, crisp, salty with a sour note, much like this song of a long-lost love from youth, remembering the good times as well as how it ended. It was part of an innovative trio of tracks from *folklore*, each one told from the perspective of a different person in a love triangle. According to Taylor, this song started with the imagery of 'a cardigan that still bears the scent of loss 20 years later'.

INGREDIENTS
2 oz. (60 ml/4 tbsp.) gold tequila
1 oz. (30 ml/2 tbsp.) Cointreau
    or triple sec
juice of half a lime
juice of half a lemon

METHOD
Shake the ingredients, then strain
    into a salt-rimmed glass and serve.

the
last great
american
daiquiri

SUGGESTED LISTENING:
the last great american dynasty

It's all about wild, carefree, decadent days epitomized by American socialite Rebekah Harkness, who once lived in Taylor's Rhode Island mansion, Holiday House. Taylor holds annual Independence Day parties at Holiday House, attended by a host of A-list celebrities. And there could be no better drink for them than this light, refreshing Daiquiri, with origins dating back to 1890s Cuba, which was all the rage in Havana in the 1930s. Beloved by Ernest Hemingway, it is perfect for alfresco enjoyment.

INGREDIENTS
2 oz. (60 ml/4 tbsp.) white rum
juice of 1 lime
1 tsp. sugar
lemon twist to garnish

METHOD
Shake the ingredients, then strain into a cocktail glass, add the garnish and serve.

mirror highball

mirrorball

We can all connect with Taylor's cry of exhaustion at trying to please everyone, likening herself to a mirrorball that endlessly spins to keep people entertained. But this cocktail doesn't need to try hard to be a crowd pleaser with its perfect blend of flavours and a knock-out trio of spirits. The flavours include orange citrus, underlying tang and a slight bitterness, while bubbles add the mirrorball sparkle.

INGREDIENTS

1 oz. (30 ml/2 tbsp.) blue Curaçao
½ oz. (15 ml/1 tbsp.) white rum
½ oz. (15 ml/1 tbsp.) gin
½ oz. (15 ml/1 tbsp.) vodka
4 oz. (120 ml/8 tbsp.) Champagne
spiral of lemon rind to garnish

METHOD

Pour the ingredients into a
    highball glass and stir.
Add the lemon rind spiral
    and serve.

mai tai ricochet

The opening choral singing on this track sets the tone of this gothic tale of an embittered lover turning up at the funeral of his object of passion. Haunting and multi-layered, the song reflected Taylor's growth as a storyteller and artist. The perfect accompaniment to this evocative track is the contrasting tropical Mai Tai which, much like the popularity of Taylor's music, has gained renown – it's become one of America's most popular cocktails.

INGREDIENTS
1 oz. (30 ml/2 tbsp.) white rum
½ oz. (15 ml/1 tbsp.) Cointreau
¼ oz. (8 ml/½ tbsp.) lime cordial
1½ oz. (45 ml/3 tbsp.) orange juice
1½ oz. (45 ml/3 tbsp.) unsweetened
    pineapple juice
splash grenadine
½ oz. (15 ml/1 tbsp.) gold rum
wedge of pineapple to garnish

METHOD
Shake the first six ingredients, then strain
    into a highball half-filled with ice.
Add the grenadine and gold rum.
Garnish with the pineapple wedge and
    serve.

august
wine
spritz

This song captures the transience of summer and a romance that slipped away like a bottle of wine. And if that rings a bell then staring into this light, golden summer in a glass, with its sweet notes and bubbles that entice then die on the tongue, might bring back fond memories of that summer love. Ideally to be enjoyed alfresco on a warm day, on a beach, by a river or on a country walk, wherever the desire takes you.

INGREDIENTS
5 seedless grapes
1 oz. (30 ml/2 tbsp.) vodka
1 tsp. honey
Prosecco

METHOD
Muddle the grapes in a shaker.
Add the vodka and honey and shake.
Strain into a champagne flute.
Fill with Prosecco and serve.

betty-ni

The classic Bellini, with its sweet peach flavour and the fizz of Champagne, is the perfect cocktail to evoke the sweet dizziness of teenage romance. In 'betty' the narrator tries to win back his childhood sweetheart after doing her wrong. Whether he was successful or not, this cocktail is sure to win you and your friends over.

INGREDIENTS
6 oz. (180 ml/12 tbsp.) white peach
    purée or peach nectar
Champagne

METHOD
Add the peach purée or nectar to
    a champagne flute, fill up with
    Champagne and serve.

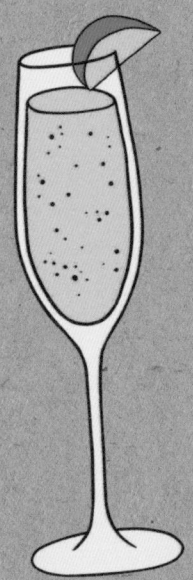

champagne
julep
problems

There is no problem at all drinking this. Refreshing, flavourful and festive but be warned, it packs a punch. Taylor wrote the ballad 'champagne problems' about an apologetic girlfriend whose personal issues led to her rejecting her boyfriend's marriage proposal. But, trust us, you will be saying 'I do, I do, I do' to this delight in a glass, in sickness and in health!

INGREDIENTS
6 fresh mint leaves
1 tsp. caster sugar
dash cognac
Champagne

METHOD
Muddle the mint and sugar with the
   cognac in a deep champagne saucer.
Fill up with Champagne and serve.

fizz the damn season

Ah, the Buck's Fizz. A cocktail it would be rude not to have at breakfast. You don't need much to make it. No need for a shaker or swizzle stick, just champers and fresh orange juice poured into a flute. The two might sound very different but when they come together, like the pair who rekindle their relationship in the song after time away, there is no denying that there is a spark.

INGREDIENTS
2 oz. (60 ml/4 tbsp.) fresh orange juice
Champagne

METHOD
Pour the orange juice into a champagne flute, fill up with Champagne and serve.

no brandy, no crime

The murder ballad she wrote as a result of her fixation with crime documentaries and podcasts is as dark and swirling as this deep and serious cognac–vermouth mix. It's about a woman named Este who a friend believes was murdered by her cheating husband and who vows to avenge her. Este is named after Este Haim, of the rock band Haim, who contributed to the track.

INGREDIENTS
2 oz. (60 ml/4 tbsp.) cognac
1 oz. (30 ml/2 tbsp.) sweet vermouth
2 dashes Angostura bitters

METHOD
Stir the cognac, vermouth and bitters in a mixing glass, then strain into a martini glass and serve.

coney island
iced tea

SUGGESTED LISTENING:
coney island

Unlike it's well-known sibling, the Long Island Iced Tea, this Coney Island version features lemon juice and cranberry instead of the lime and cola, offering a fruity alternative that still packs an alcoholic punch! A classic, like the rhythmic waltz tempo throughout this haunting tune which sees Taylor duet with Matt Berninger, lead vocalist of the band The National, about a separated couple's memories in Coney Island.

INGREDIENTS

1 oz. (30 ml/2 tbsp.) vodka
1 oz. (30 ml/2 tbsp.) triple sec
1 oz. (30 ml/2 tbsp.) gold tequila
1 oz. (30 ml/2 tbsp.) light rum
1 oz. (30 ml/2 tbsp.) gin
1 oz. (30 ml/2 tbsp.) fresh lemon juice
1 oz. (30 ml/2 tbsp.) gomme syrup
cranberry juice

METHOD

Shake the ingredients, except
   the cranberry juice.
Strain into an ice-filled
   highball glass.
Fill up with cranberry juice, stir and serve.

long story shot

SUGGESTED LISTENING:
long story short

Get the girls round to enjoy what is, to cut a long story short, essentially a pineapple upside down cake in a glass! Oh so sweet, with a lovely creamy, yellow colour, it will give you a sugar rush like never before. Direct and straight to the point, like the lyrics in this song about Taylor finding solace with her then boyfriend Joe Alwyn after her feud with Kanye West and final resolution that she has found peace and confidence once more.

INGREDIENTS
½ oz. (15 ml/1 tbsp.) Bailey's
½ oz. (15 ml/1 tbsp.) vodka
½ oz. (15 ml/1 tbsp.) butterscotch
    schnapps
½ oz. (15 ml/1 tbsp.) pineapple juice

METHOD
 Stir the ingredients in a mixing glass,
    then strain into a shot glass and serve.

Lavender Hazy

This bubbly blue cocktail, sweetly orange in taste, will leave you in a heady haze of delight. The fresh lemon and Champagne help lift it beyond your dreams. The phrase 'lavender haze' was one that intrigued Taylor after she heard it mentioned in an episode of *Mad Men*. She used it to describe the dizzy state of being in love and too many of this delicious cocktail are sure to have a similar effect!

INGREDIENTS
1 oz. (30 ml/2 tbsp.) blue Curaçao
1 oz. (30 ml/2 tbsp.) Cointreau
Champagne

METHOD
Pour the blue Curaçao and Cointreau
   into a highball glass.
Fill with Champagne and serve.

Sloe on the Beach

SUGGESTED LISTENING:
Snow on the Beach

The beach is an ideal spot to look up to the stars in wonder and the best place to drink this hauntingly red, sweet cocktail, originally called the Eclipse and created by famed bartender Harry Craddock to celebrate the 1927 total solar eclipse in Britain. Just as in the song about two people falling in love simultaneously, with background vocals from Lana Del Rey, this is just the start of your love affair with the drink!

INGREDIENTS
1 olive
dash grenadine
1 oz. (30 ml/2 tbsp.) sloe gin
1 oz. (30 ml/2 tbsp.) gin
dash fresh lemon juice

METHOD
Put the olive in a martini glass and cover with the grenadine.
Shake the two types of gin and lemon, strain into the glass, not disturbing the grenadine, and serve.

Midnight
Champagne

SUGGESTED LISTENING:
Midnight Rain

Champagne is a recurring theme in Tay's songs and the classic bubbly makes this sparkling concoction with a gorgeous blue-green colour, like an ocean at twilight. It combines the sweet and tangy flavours of citrus with the refreshing fizz. Full of drama and passion like the message in this song about choosing career and fame over a comfortable domestic life, despite the pain that you have to go through to get there. Just like this drink, good things come to those who strive for the best.

INGREDIENTS
dash amaretto
dash blue Curaçao
dash fresh lemon juice
Champagne

METHOD
Pour the first three ingredients into a champagne flute, stir, then fill with Champagne and serve.

Vigilante
Shot

Feeling moody and like you want to get your own back on someone? Ready for payback time? Well, revenge is best served velvety smooth with this semi-sweet, intense raspberry-flavoured tipple with a hidden punch. Known for its vibrant purple colour, it's as dark as the tone of the song which takes aim at a former lover and recruits his ex-wife to join her in her deadly plot.

INGREDIENTS
1 oz. (30 ml/2 tbsp.) citrus vodka
½ oz. (15 ml/1 tbsp.) triple sec
½ oz. (15 ml/1 tbsp.) Chambord

METHOD
Shake the ingredients, then strain
into a shot glass and serve.

Karma-pirinha

Never mind those who have wronged you – the universe has a way of setting everything right in the end. Taylor performed 'Karma' as the closing song during her Eras Tour, ending with a bang, a dazzling fireworks display and an explosion of confetti. 'Karma is the guy on the Chiefs', she sang in reference to her boyfriend, Travis Kelce, of the Kansas City Chiefs. A caipirinha, the national drink of Brazil will also put you in the party spirit. Cachaça is all about samba and carnival. Add lime, sugar and ice and get moving to the beat with your amigos!

INGREDIENTS
1 lime
3 sugar lumps
2 oz. (60 ml/4 tbsp.) cachaça

METHOD
Cut the lime into eighths, then muddle
  with the sugar in an old-fashioned
  glass.
Fill the glass with crushed ice and
  pour in the cachaça. Stir and serve.

Sweet Vermouth Nothing

'Sweet Nothing' explores how the seemingly inconsequential and mundane things actually mean the world. In this cocktail, the sweetness of the vermouth subtly cuts through the dominant Grand Marnier and kick of gin, lending a pleasing, lasting tranquillity to the senses. Like Taylor, this will be one to rush home for in moments of madness.

INGREDIENTS
2 oz. (60 ml/4 tbsp.) Grand Marnier
1 oz. (30 ml/2 tbsp.) gin
1 oz. (30 ml/2 tbsp.) dry vermouth
½ oz. (15 ml/1 tbsp.) sweet vermouth
dash Angostura bitters

METHOD
Shake the ingredients, then strain
    into a martini glass and serve.

The Great Wallbanger

SUGGESTED LISTENING:
The Great War

While this fighting song explores the conflict which comes at the end of a relationship, this sweet and fruity cocktail offers the antidote to the turmoil. In the 70s, there was no more popular cocktail than the Harvey Wallbanger as it was the perfect drink for a good time with friends, just what you need when your relationship is on the rocks!

INGREDIENTS
2 oz. (60 ml/4 tbsp.) vodka
5 oz. (150 ml/10 tbsp.) fresh orange
    juice
1 oz. (30 ml/2 tbsp.) Galliano
slice of orange to garnish

METHOD
Pour the vodka and orange juice
    into an ice-filled highball and stir.
Float the Galliano on top.
Garnish with the orange and serve with
    a stirrer.

INDEX

Basics section and cocktail recipes © Carlton Books Limited 2024
General introduction and cocktail recipe introductions ©Headline Publishing Group Limited 2024
Illustrations ©Headline Publishing Group Limited 2024

First published in 2024 by Welbeck
An Imprint of HEADLINE PUBLISHING GROUP

1

Cataloguing in Publication Data is available from the British Library

ISBN 9781035419869

Printed and bound in China

Headline's policy is to use papers that are natural, renewable and recyclable products and made from wood grown in well-managed forests and other controlled sources. The logging and manufacturing processes are expected to conform to the environmental regulations of the country of origin.

HEADLINE PUBLISHING GROUP
An Hachette UK Company
Carmelite House
50 Victoria Embankment
London EC4Y 0DZ

www.headline.co.uk
www.hachette.co.uk

The basics section and cocktail recipes in this book originally appeared in *The Complete Bartender's Guide* by Dave Broom, first published in 2003.